Herbert Krause

Boise State University Western Writers Series   Number 66

Herbert Krause

By Arthur R. Huseboe

Augustana College

Sioux Falls, South Dakota

Editors: Wayne Chatterton
James H. Maguire

Business Manager:
James Hadden

Cover Design and Illustration
by Arny Skov, Copyright 1985

Boise State University, Boise, Idaho

Copyright 1985
by the
Boise State University Western Writers Series

ALL RIGHTS RESERVED

Library of Congress Card No. 85-70126

International Standard Book No. 0-88430-040-4

Printed in the United States of America by
Boise State University Printing and Graphics Services
Boise, Idaho

Herbert Krause

I

By all the measurements that matter Herbert Krause is a Western American writer: he was born in the West along the western edge of Minnesota where the rough terrain of Pockerbrush slides downhill into the wheat-rich Red River valley and beyond—and he wrote about the West in all his work—three novels, two plays, fistfulls of poems, and speeches, essays, chapters, and introductions. It's true that when he received his first literary prize he called himself a Midwestern writer, but that was in Chicago and before he'd thought very much about the matter. By the time his second novel appeared, Krause had come to a clear sense of where the West was—it was trans-Mississippi and it extended deep into Old Mexico to the south and far into Canada to the north. He considered himself very much a part of it.

Krause's first novel, *Wind Without Rain* (1939), is a highly poetic work, transmuting the base metal of everyday farm life in western Minnesota—the mud and dust and snow and the interminable labor—into the gold of metaphor and simile. The next two novels moved farther west in their subject matter, while remaining well within the area that Hamlin Garland has labeled the Middle Border and that Frederick Manfred has called Siouxland. From its starting point in the wooded hills north of Fergus Falls, the first of these, *The Thresher* (1946), spills over into the wheat fields of North and South Dakota, and it succeeds as the most accurate and most persuasive fictional account of the era of steam-powered threshing in America. The last of Krause's novels, *The Oxcart Trail* (1954), includes nearly all of the themes familiar to readers of Western American writing: the flight from the law, the life of a raw frontier village, the rigorous overland trek in covered wagons (oxcarts in this case), skirmishes with Indians, and even the love affair between the frontiersman and the school teacher. The most interesting of Krause's themes, however, are those that are found in the first two novels, those that relate to the hard life of German immigrant settlers on the frontier, their slow and grudging adjustments to the dominant American culture, their harsh religion, their folkways, and their suspicious resentment of budding artistic talent.

It is possible to find in Krause's early life and youth the seeds that were to grow into these pervasive topics in his novels. As a youngster he had a precocious interest in metaphoric language and in powerful images, or so he believed. He wrote intuitively, instinctively, like the young Alexander Pope, lisping in numbers as a child "for the numbers came." As a youth he sketched out stories, urged to do so by listening to his blacksmith father spin yarns of the old times around Fergus Falls but shamed as well when that same father laughed at his early efforts and at his ambition. Spinning yarns was one thing, Art Krause believed, but writing was another matter. Above all, certainly, Krause wanted to write as a means of escape from the narrow confines of his own impoverished and solidly German background and of the hill country that he later called Pockerbrush.

During his college days at St. Olaf, Northfield, Minnesota, Krause came to realize the possibilities of telling the story of the German-Americans in western Minnesota just as Ole Rølvaag had told the story of the Norwegians in eastern South Dakota. The Rølvaag name, as a matter of fact, had helped to entice Krause to attend St. Olaf, although the two men never met and Rølvaag died shortly after Krause's arrival on campus. In letters to friends Krause referred to the novelist as one of his inspirations, and in a student essay he bemoaned the fact that there was not a Rølvaag to interpret the German Lutheran heritage sympathetically and accurately. When *Wind Without Rain* appeared, it seemed to many critics, including Rølvaag's own translator, Lincoln Colcord, that Krause might be a worthy successor to the Norwegian-American novelist. And the appearance of *The Thresher* eight years later called forth renewed comparisons between the two. James Gray, literary editor of the *Chicago Daily News* and himself a novelist, was one of the many who saw Krause as the equal of Rølvaag. Gray's review in early 1947, in fact, was headlined, "Herbert Krause Takes Mantle of O.E. Rølvaag."

II

The man who created Pockerbrush was born on 25 May 1905 on a small farm in Otter Tail County in west central Minnesota, ten miles north-northeast of Fergus Falls. The township of his birth, Friberg, had been given that name in 1874 by the German settlers in the area. His parents were farmers, offspring of immigrants from Saxony and Mecklenburg and elsewhere in Germany. Father Arthur Krause was first a farmer and then a blacksmith, and young Herbert grew up to the sound of steam engine and gasoline tractor, of hammer and anvil echoing through the valley. His mother Bertha was the daughter of one of the early German settlers, Carl Peters, who had come to the U.S. from Mecklenburg some time in the 1860s. Carl's name and that of Grandfather Adolph Krause are among those of the fourteen men who founded Immanuel Lutheran congregation of Friberg in 1873 and who built the first log church the next year.

Herbert's parents, then, were born and grew up as near neighbors in a community bound closely together by their German ancestry and language and by their Lutheran faith. They first met as teenagers, as Herbert recalled the story, when Arthur drove five miles to a neighbor's for seed and found a blue-eyed girl pumping water in the yard. The two were married by Pastor George Matzat at Immanuel in December 1903 and set up housekeeping on Arthur's "fifty," a mile away from Grandpa Krause's place. The first of six children, Herbert, was born seventeen months later, Dr. George Kugler attending.

Growing up in Friberg was an unusually intense experience for young Herbert. His was a deeply sensitive nature, alert to the wide range of beauty and of suffering in human life and in the nature around him. He was small for his age, a runt he called himself years later, and he usually got the worst of it in neighborhood tussles. Those altercations helped to sharpen his sensitivity to unfair treatment and his skill in vituperation—both so evident in his novels and essays and in his later correspondence—for whenever he lost a fight, which was almost always, he would stand at a distance and hurl imprecations at his tormentor.

Besides being the neighborhood runt, with a ready temper and proud nature, Krause stood out as different among the children of the neighborhood because of his intellectual precocity. His love of words developed rapidly after he entered school at age six-and-a-half and learned to read English well. His most deeply moving discovery in the early years at Wolf Lake school was E.D.E.N. Southworth's *Ishmael; or, In the Depths*, and his most difficult learning experience was the memorizing of poetry. In the pages of *Ishmael* and its successor *Self-Raised* the young Krause found a way to escape the personal dilemma in which he found himself—his frustrating feelings of inferiority (Upton 3-5). As young as he was—perhaps only seven or eight at the time—Krause was acutely aware that the fates had stacked the deck against him: he was poor, physically unimpressive, the son of simple German farmers, and isolated from the rest of the world by heritage and geography. For Ishmael, similarly disadvantaged, an education could be the way out—if one possessed merit and if one cultivated high principles. So it had been for Ishmael and so it would be for Herbert Krause.

If education was to be an escape from the hard life of farming or blacksmithing, there would have to be much more beyond the ten years of rural school available to Krause in Friberg township, but it would have to wait until he could pay his own way. Krause's efforts to teach himself to write short stories and poetry, consequently, were discouraged by his impoverished parents. His enrolling in the Short Story Department of the Hoosier Institute (a mail-order school in Fort Wayne, Indiana) they considered frivolous, and they frowned even on his purchase of magazines. In his journal for 1935 Krause recalled "the dreadful moment when Dad, after paying the mail man for a *Cosmopolitan* I begged for and finally got, rebuked me by saying quietly, as he calmly picked up a load of fire-wood we were getting, 'Well, Son, you'd have done better, getting a pair of socks.' The shame and agony of that moment remains with me to this moment. If he had raged, but no." After all, his father asked the sixteen-year-old Herbert, what was there to write about in Friberg?

III

In October 1926 Herbert Krause entered the academy division of Park Region Luther College, a small Norwegian Lutheran Synod school in Fergus Falls. He entered at twenty-one and one-half years old, still scrawny and still with a chip on his shoulder, and with plans in mind to write a long poem about a son in rebellion against his father. That project was never completed, but over the next several years the topic of the brutally dominant father and the rebellious son crops up again and again: in drafts of poems and stories to be found among the Krause Papers at Augustana College, Sioux Falls, South Dakota, in two or three early published verses, in his one-act play *Bondsmen to the Hills* and the outline of a long story, *Franz Vildvogel* (these latter two begun in 1933), and in *Wind Without Rain* and *The Thresher*. Whatever the sources of Krause's interest in the theme—and certainly the long delay in his education, the oppression of his German-Lutheran religion, and the poverty of his family formed part of his bitterness—it is the most persistent and powerful motif in his writing, more powerful even than his deep love for the intricate beauty of nature.

Throughout his first three years at Park Region, Krause continued to scribble verses, as he liked to put it, and to write in his journal. One of his classmates recalled with fondness how Krause used to come to his and "Squirt" Olson's room to visit, "And sometimes you would have a poem," wrote the friend to Herbert, "or a short story for us that you had worked out" (Newman B. Olsgaard to Krause, 3 March 1947). The first fruit of his "working out" of poetry appeared in the school paper, *The Hilltop Crier* (19 October 1927). It was a technically complex lyric called "Autumn Days," marred only occasionally by poeticisms and pathetic fallacies, and decidedly promising. The twenty-four lines concluded,

> October days were dearer than many summer ones.
> November days are clearer, aglow with frosty suns.
> Soft Autumn days are hazy, and all on pleasure bent—
> I love their current, lazy and full of sweet content.

On the other hand, the dark and brooding side of Krause's nature is reflected in "The Mountain," a poetic character sketch that appeared in *The Hilltop Crier* on 20 February 1929. Besides being the most ambitious of the pieces that Krause published during his academy days, it picked up the theme of the domineering father that had obsessed him two-and-a-half years earlier and developed it into the sketch of a poor mountain woman, oppressed by hard work and poverty, and brutalized by a drunken husband who has crippled their daughter by throwing her against the wall. The hopelessness of the wife's situation foreshadows that of the gloomiest passages in *Wind Without Rain*, *The Thresher*, and his collection of poems *Neighbor Boy*; and it reflects the deep pessimism that frequently burdened Krause's heart and mind, pessimism that can be seen in his first real diary, begun the previous winter: "My desire, my paramount dream, burns within me like a white-hot fire, searing me, burning my brain, threatening to consume my heart, to incinerate my whole being. And what can I do? What, oh, what? Nothing."

Despite the occasional gloom of his diaries and letters, Krause entered his last year at Park Region with enthusiasm. To one of his favorite teachers, Alma Karstad, then dean of women at Midland College, he wrote of his plans for the year after graduation. He would teach for $65 a month in a parochial school at Annandale, Minnesota, where William D. Kanning, his home pastor, was now serving. In the meantime, he continued to write and to publish poetry and prose in *The Hilltop Crier*. With each success his confidence grew. As "chapel editor" he produced a dozen prose pieces that summed up the chapel sermons throughout the year. And he also tried his hand at light satiric essays: a piece on yo-yoing and one on the "terrible effects of work" in which he pledged to give up smoking and Mickey Mouse movies.

As a climax to his success, he learned that two of his poems would appear in print in national magazines, "Judean Night" in *The Lutheran Herald* (published 15 December 1931), and "The Telephone" in *The Parchment* (University of Kansas, January 1932). This latter was a free-verse narrative of 163 lines, somewhat florid in diction but realized with dramatic intensity. The young woman, peeling potatoes in the cellar and musing over her family and fiancé and impending wedding, does not hear the repeated ringing of the telephone upstairs. When she does and rushes to it,

> She stopped in the doorway, a thousand thoughts
> like a horde of ravening fiends, hell-haunted,
> Jim falling into the glittering death . . . .
> No, no; it couldn't be that . . . very likely
> it was Mrs. Daniels, asking about
> the length of the hem of the wedding dress.

And so on, through more fears and mild concerns, until the last line:

> She lifted the receiver and heard . . . . what?

The editor of *The Parchment* wrote to Krause's teacher, Ragnild Quien, calling the long narrative "rather tremendous" and asking where Krause intended to continue his studies. As his confidence as a writer grew over the 1930-31 school year, so did his ambition. With the encouragement of Miss Quien and many others he decided to apply to St. Olaf College, Northfield, Minnesota. He entered in the fall, eager to study at Ole Rølvaag's institution.

Without doubt, however, the luckiest personal attachment that Krause made during the years he spent at St. Olaf was not to Rølvaag but to Professor George Weida Spohn (1879-1943), chairman of the English department and Krause's academic advisor. He was something of a surprise for Krause, because the young writer had travelled down to St. Olaf expecting to be impressed by certain great educators and writers. Ole Rølvaag he put at the top of the list, with C. A. Mellby (history), Julius Boraas (education), and F.

Melius Christianson (music) following after. As it turned out, Krause never met Rølvaag in the two months before the novelist's death (Ragnild Quien to Krause, 23 Oct. 1931), and Boraas gave him the first C+ he'd ever received. So much for two of the giants. But Spohn quickly earned Krause's respect and trust.

For three years "Pop" Spohn was Krause's mentor, during his junior and senior years there and during the annus mirabilis 1933-34 when Krause was assistant to the librarian by day and poet, playwright, and novelist by night. Besides his library work, he audited French, acted in several plays, and taught Sunday school. Amid these activities he wrote in outline form the first sixty-one pages of *Franz Vildvogel*, which would turn out to be the novel *Wind Without Rain*. That spring, moreover, under the direction of Ella Rølvaag, daughter of the novelist, his one-act tragedy *Bondsmen to the Hills* was produced in Ytterboe Auditorium to great applause and floods of tears.

The concentrated tension of the play is a foreshadowing of the many moments of emotional pain in Krause's first novel, *Wind Without Rain*. Like young Krause himself, Benny is encouraged to go to high school by his teacher and his mother, but his father, insensitive to the beauty in Pockerbrush, ridicules his son when he catches him writing poetry and finally drives him to running with a neighborhood gang of toughs. At the denouement of the play, word comes that Benny has been shot to death. The mother is devastated; even the father comes close to breaking, but the aged grandfather provides the greatest dramatic tension in the story, uttering mournful warnings from time to time throughout the play like a Greek chorus, until—just before word of Benny's death arrives—he pronounces the prophetic line, "The hand of the Lord reaches out and strikes." The audience wept throughout, Krause reported, and actress Thorra Brekken, who played the browbeaten mother, cried so hard afterwards that she couldn't be stopped for ten minutes. Although *Bondsmen to the Hills* was never published, it went on to win the first-place gold cup at the Midwestern Folk Drama Tournament at Cape Girardeau, Missouri. It was, Krause wrote to a friend, "the luckiest thing that ever happened to an undeserving Pockerbrusher."

IV

In the fall of 1934 Krause entered the University of Iowa. The academic program that drew him there was a novelty on the American educational and literary scene, a graduate school where one could earn both the M.A. and the Ph.D. degrees with works of creative writing in place of the usual scholarly thesis or dissertation. Two of its graduates had won early distinction: Paul Engle (M.A. 1932) had offered the collection of poems *One Slim Feather* as his thesis; under the title *Worn Earth* it was the first thesis of poems to be published. His second collection of poems, *American Song*, was published by Doubleday in 1934 and enthusiastically reviewed in the *New York Times*. Wallace Stegner, who also earned the M.A. in 1932 for creative writing, would win the Little, Brown $2,500 novelette prize in 1937 with *Remembering Laughter*. Krause's ardent wish was that his collection of Pockerbrush poems might help gain him an M.A. and perhaps literary recognition to boot, and "Pop" Spohn joined him in that hope: "Keep up the fighting spirit," he wrote to Krause, "and some day you will flash upon the front page of the *New York Times* as Paul Engle did" (23 Nov. 1934).

Krause's self-confidence was deeply shaken that spring, however, when his efforts to publish his M.A. thesis, a collection of poems called *Pockerbrush*, were unsuccessful. A number of those poems appeared in 1939 in *Neighbor Boy* and are discussed below, but at least for the first time Krause could put into print in a prefatory note his definition of Pockerbrush: "a country of tangled undergrowth in that region of western Minnesota where the hills shrink away from the broad 'flats' of the Red River Valley."

In April Krause learned that he had won a summer scholarship to the Bread Loaf School of English and that he had also won third prize from Galleon Press for one of his poems. Bread Loaf was the best news, of course. The most exciting part of the six weeks there was his meeting such writers as Dorothy Canfield Fisher, Theodore Morrison, Stephen Vincent Benét, and Robert Frost. These last two especially impressed Krause, both Pulitzer Prize winning poets and both encouraging. Krause wrote to his mother: "Met Frost, the greatest poet in America today and he likes Pockerbrush." Frost, in turn, kept track of Krause through their mutual friend Charles Foster, also a graduate student at Iowa, and in early 1937 Frost wrote a warmly supportive letter to Krause, asking him to bring something to read the next summer. Benét was to be even more supportive. When Krause had only a few pages of his first novel completed, Benét read them and was enthusiastic enough to offer to recommend the completed work to his own publisher. His comments, when he did see the finished book, were selected by Bobbs-Merrill as the most powerful statement of the importance of *Wind Without Rain*: "I think it marks the first step in the work of a man who is going to be one of our essential writers."

From the fall of 1935 through the fall of 1937 Krause dug at the coursework for the Ph.D. degree with typical assiduity, taught freshman composition, and assisted Hubert Hoeltje in his research work on Ralph Waldo Emerson's journals. But in the summers and at odd moments he labored at a novel based on the Vildvogel story he had sketched out at St. Olaf. Under the direction of Edwin Ford

Piper and with the encouragement of Norman Foerster, who had designed the innovative degree program at Iowa, Krause hoped to produce a piece that would be publishable as well. Indeed, one of Foerster's expectations from the beginning in 1931 was that, besides becoming thoroughly acquainted with traditional approaches to understanding literature, students who chose to specialize in imaginative writing should publish their work "under reputable auspices" (Stephen Wilburs 44-46). Until 1938, in fact, as Wilburs notes, only three works, one of them a novel — David Ash's *Liberty Hall*—had been submitted as creative doctoral dissertations. In March of that year, however, the *Cedar Rapids Gazette* announced that four students in the School of Letters had had their novels accepted for publication. Krause was among them.

When *Wind Without Rain* was published by Bobbs-Merrill in February of 1939, it created a national sensation and Krause was lionized throughout the Midwest in a series of autograph parties, radio interviews, and readings. By mid-March the novel was listed as a best seller by both the *New York Herald Tribune* and the *Chicago Daily News.* For the most part critics and reviewers received the book with astonishment. Few of them, to be sure, paid much attention to the ethnic concerns of the novel or to the explicit criticism of the narrowly fundamental Lutheranism practiced in the Hills. Instead it was the rich intensity of the poetry that impressed them, as well as the atmosphere of gloom that pervaded every chapter.

Of all the reviews, Krause read most avidly those in *The Saturday Review of Literature, The New York Times, Newsweek,* and *The New Yorker.* The *Saturday Review* piece had been done by Wallace Stegner at the urging of another of Krause's Iowa mentors, Wilbur Schramm, and it was almost uniformly enthusiastic. For all of its tragic disillusionment, said Stegner, *Wind Without Rain* was a very beautiful novel, sometimes in its narrative material but more often in the "how" of its writing. "We have waited a long time," he wrote, "for a writer who could, without compromising in the least the integrity of his observation, or softening his picture of the world, still transmute that real world into beauty." Privately, Stegner confided to Krause that the last twenty pages were "overloaded with pathos," but, he wrote, "You'll be compared with Vardis Fisher in a review or two" (Letter to Krause 23 Jan. 1939). Margaret Wallace in the *Times* found almost all of the novel's qualities to be in excess: Krause's Pockerbrush is less a place than "some peculiarly joyless and tortured realm of the mind." And yet, "his way of writing is his own—febrile, poetic, with something of the incantatory quality which first surprised us in the work of Thomas Wolfe, but without Wolfe's variety." *Newsweek*'s review, by Burton Rascoe, called *Wind Without Rain* the best novel of the season, notable for its lyricism and idiomatic Americanese, but too intensely pessimistic. Clifton Fadiman's review in *The New Yorker*, while finding occasional power and conviction in Krause's novel, deplored "the bits of fine writing that stud his prose like cheap jewelry." Fadiman's review was especially stinging because it ridiculed the poetry that Krause felt gave the novel its real strength. But the review was ironic as well, for Fadiman had served as one of the editors at Simon and Schuster who had given high praise to the early draft of *Wind Without Rain*. In the publisher's report to Krause in mid-December 1936, Maria Leiper had summed up the conclusions of the four editors: Krause is a real writer, a genuine talent, well above the average.

Consequently, when Krause received the $1,000 Friends of American Writers Award at the Palmer House in Chicago on 16 March (with fellow Minnesotan Sinclair Lewis and other dignitaries in attendance), he had the peculiar pleasure of hearing Fadiman, the featured speaker, publicly name Krause among the most brilliant of young American novelists. At the same time, Fadiman warned that most writers don't develop beyond their first successful efforts. "We have the most talented young writers in the world," he said. "That is the trouble. Sinclair Lewis has written many good books, and many bad books, but he continues to grow" ("First Novel" 22). Krause responded on behalf of Midwestern writers who were telling as honestly as they knew how of the men and women who are born and bred in the Midwest and remain there despite dust storms and blizzards and other destructive forces. The moment was as sweet as any Krause would have the rest of his life.

In addition to the critical response nationwide, of equal concern to Krause was the reaction of his neighbors and relatives back around Fergus Falls, the Pockerbrushers whose frailties he had so lyrically laid bare. While in public he denied persistently that *Wind Without Rain* was in any way autobiographical, the truth was that the inspiration for the Franz Vildvogel story he had sketched out at St. Olaf in 1933 had been a man named Drager from the Friberg area, and many of the episodes in the completed novel were clearly drawn from Krause's own life experiences. A few weeks after the novel appeared, for example, the pastor from Krause's university days announced his amazement at the autobiographical details he had discovered in the first forty-three pages of *Wind Without Rain*: "In the story of your life which you gave me at various times in our little church at Iowa City I find many scenes and circumstances which are reproduced in your novel. I do hope you did not find the model for the Lutheran Pastor in a certain *Julius A. Friedrich* . . . . Let us hope the readers will not judge the Lutheran ministry and the Lutheran Church as a whole by that Minnesota pastor and his 'Gemeinde.'"

Back in Pockerbrush the reaction was predictable. Krause's

young friend John Clifford Danielson wrote to tell him that the Methodist Church ladies had purchased *Wind Without Rain* for the Sunday School, probably because the advertising laid emphasis on Krause's knowledge of the King James version of the Bible. But now the book had mysteriously disappeared. The following Christmas at Immanuel Lutheran Church, Krause noted a decided lack of neighborliness. "I didn't find much of that," he wrote to a friend, "and it hurt a little, even though I should be used to it by this time. I never saw so many backs turned in my direction at church—never before." Lincoln Colcord's prediction was coming true: "I suspect your book will be anathema to the majority opinion of your people in the region. You will catch hell for it" (24 Feb. 1939).

What Krause had intended was a good deal more than mere revenge for a lifetime of injuries suffered at the hands of many in Pockerbrush, although some of his friends at Iowa recalled the harsh things he had said there about the people of his community. To Robert Whitehand, one of his fellow novelists at Iowa City, he wrote: "All of those 'grudges,' as you call them, were burnt out of me in the years following graduation—years at the graduate school and the search for a job. I see my people now in a different light—I see their struggle. The roughness that comes not from a nature inherently cantankerous but warped into that shape by relentless acres and endless furrows, you see." Nothing about the novel is more true than that it is a powerful evocation of those acres and of the stultifying effects of endless labor and few rewards on the sensitive spirit.

The story of *Wind Without Rain* is that of two men. The stronger of them is Johan Vildvogel, who years before had fled from a northern lumber camp under mysterious circumstances and is grudgingly accepted by the Pockerbrush community. His marriage to a shy orphan named Minna results in four sons: Walter, Fritzie,

Jepthah, and Franz. With these four and his wife under his thumb, Old Vildvogel strives to scrape a living from his scant acres. The whole family is in constant fear of him, and that fear is deepened by the fire-and-brimstone preaching of Pastor Sunnenbaum and the relentless pressure of the Bank, always as ready to gobble up their acres as Satan is to seize their souls.

Young Franz is the other center of attention in the novel. His sensitive and passionate love of music is brutally thwarted by his father and the Pastor—until Old Vildvogel discovers that Franz can make money with his fiddle-playing and reluctantly allows him to perform at local dances. In the midst of the family's life-and-death struggle with the soil, Franz accidentally injures Jeppy while they are out sledding, and he must add to his other sufferings the knowledge that he has crippled his brother. Yet Franz continues to practice the violin and to play, teaching himself in idle moments and finding in the music a powerful anodyne for pain.

As the seasons pass, first Walter and then Fritz run away from home and their father's fierce domination. Mother Minna dies one summer, exhausted by the hard life they have led. Only on her death-bed does she learn from Pastor Sunnenbaum the story of Johan's jailing up north, before their marriage, and of the shame that has goaded him ever since. Not long after, Old Vildvogel is permanently crippled, and Franz marries Tinkla Bauer instead of the blonde flirt Liliem Schoen whom he has loved all his life. So the stuff of tragedy continues to spin out for the family. Vildvogel dies at last and the family moves to a better farm, but Franz's persistent love for Liliem leads to still another death and to the certainty that the cycle of brutal father and rebellious son has begun again in the Vildvogel family.

There are other strongly drawn characters peopling *Wind Without Rain*. The Lutheran pastor Sunnenbaum is a caricature of the wrath-breathing pastors whom Krause had heard in the Hills and who symbolized for him the dark excesses of Missouri Synod doctrine. The two girls—the vivacious Liliem, driven by a desire for a life more agreeable than that of a dirt-farmer's wife; and Tinkla, robust and patient, willing to take Franz on the rebound (as she must, under the circumstances)—these two contribute to the bewildering chain of suffering that is Franz Vildvogel's life in Pockerbrush. Perhaps the most interesting of all, however, is Jepthah Vildvogel, the narrator of *Wind Without Rain* and Franz's admirer despite the accident. It is Jeppy's voice that narrates the whole of the novel as he looks back in memory from some distant hospital, a "white interlude of peace" that enables him to see with clarity that poverty, a harsh climate, and a harsh religion have made a sad waste of human life in Pockerbrush. It was the voice of Krause himself, looking back from the shelter of the University of Iowa at the deep pain that he had tried so fervently to escape.

Out of these same sources Krause wrote two short stories that appeared in the 1940s. The earlier of the two, "Horning in the Fall," is little more than an unplotted sketch, a scene that might have been included in *Wind Without Rain*. It is an emotionally taut occasion in Pockerbrush with neighbors watching the bloody and painful business of de-horning cattle; there is a jealous young woman in the crowd, being advised to use magic to win her man; and there are vignettes of the German folk of the valley, with snatches of conversation and clusters of metaphors for flavoring. "The Oak Tree" is more successful as a plotted short story, and once again a Pockerbrush farm is the setting. A young couple, having struggled with rented land the first year of their marriage, at last can afford an eighty of their own. But the husband, lured by better places to rent, doesn't share his wife's fierce desire for their own farm. When she dies that same year, he makes up his mind to leave farming altogether and find a job and learn city ways.

V

In the long interval between *Wind Without Rain* and the publication in 1947 of his second novel, *The Thresher*, Krause busied himself at publishing his poems, at teaching, and at gathering material about the era of the steam threshing machine. Even though his salary was only $1,800 a year, his newly acquired teaching position at Augustana College gave him as much pleasure as his first novel. When he had signed the contract in January 1938, the year before *Wind Without Rain* appeared, he had written in delight to his best friend John Clifford Danielson: "Now the Divine Maker has dropped this bushel of luck, pressed down and running over, into my hands. I can scarcely believe it." "Yesterday, by the magic of a drop of ink and two hen-scratches on a bit of paper, I became the head of the English Department at Augustana College, Sioux Falls, South Dakota. (Such a grand roll those syllables have.) I am to establish a division of creative writing, by which means I hope young men and women of that region will be encouraged to preserve the heritage of their forefathers, in song and drama, poetry and prose."

In the summer of 1939 Krause enjoyed still another triumph: he returned to Iowa City to take part as one of the faculty in the Writers Conference there. There he rubbed shoulders with the likes of Ruth Suckow and John G. Neihardt, with his former teachers Foerster and Schramm, and with his former fellow student and teacher Paul Engle. Piper had died a few weeks before, unhappily, but Krause was elated at being able to spend three days with Robert Frost, and he took the opportunity as well to begin planning with Norman

Froiland of Midland House in Iowa City for the publication that fall of his book of poems *Neighbor Boy*.

The delay in the writing of the second novel, despite the urging of his publisher, is easily explained, for it resulted from the same combination of circumstances that prevented Krause from ever taking his qualifying exams at Iowa, that last hurdle between him and the doctorate. On the one hand the long struggle to find a teaching job was over and Krause at age thirty-three was at last able to enjoy the respect and even adulation that had so long eluded him. On the other hand he had by no means escaped entirely the poverty that had plagued him all his life. Besides the ongoing responsibility he felt, as eldest son, toward his mother and the rest of the family, he owed money to everybody in 1939, or so it seemed, to Foerster and other friends, to his aunt Mary, and to the insurance company; and he still owed a heavy debt for his Park Region education, a grand total of $2,322 (a small fortune in the 1930s). With the Park Region debt, of course, he was fortunate, because in 1931 his psychology teacher N. L. Fadness had taken over the total amount, nearly $500, and with patience and compassion carried Krause until December 1947, when proceeds from *The Thresher* enabled Krause to pay him back and be entirely free of debt for the first time in his life.

When *Neighbor Boy* appeared late in 1939, Krause attained still another of his long-deferred ambitions, for he had been scribbling at poetry since his Park Region days and had amassed over a hundred poems, some of them having appeared already in periodicals and anthologies. But the thirty-nine poems in *Neighbor Boy* were not meant as a collection of all of Krause's pieces, for whatever reason. Some of the fine lyrics that he had included in his master's thesis were omitted, perhaps because of personal preference, perhaps because of space limitations. Those he did print, including some that were written specifically for the collection, give the impression—taken together—of a smaller and paler version of *Wind Without Rain*. Here are short narrative and dramatic sketches, reminiscent of Frost, certainly, and of Edwin Ford Piper, both Krause's poetic mentors. But the names of the characters are different, Pockerbrush names all: Biedermann, Kethmann, Bursch, Glugersfeld, Poger, and Kickenbutt; and the subjects—drought, a barn dance, a beaten horse, the second coming at Pilversack's, country conversations about weather and the neighbors—all are characteristically Krause.

The dramatic sketches in particular display the terse conversations and rural metaphors that Krause had heard and recorded in Pockerbrush. In "Burned Out" the cattle are "drum-tight, nosin' for water, hardly fit to kill," and young Biedermann has "chewed his cud of dirt longer than most." One of the speakers in "Burned Out" concludes:

>God, how a man breaks up in pieces
>When his belly's empty and he's down.
>I brought a sack of feed for him—
>Week or two ago. He hunched right down
>On the barn floor and cried.

In "The Sky's Too Far Away" the country poet complains that nobody in the valley appreciates his efforts to capture the beauty of nature. His friend replies, with an eye to the beauty the poet doesn't see:

>*You* catch "the sky's gold out of sunset."
>But a dozen sundowns never set Old Kethmann's eyes
>Afire like a "twenty acre" well-manured.

The rapid conversational exchanges in "The Second Coming up in Pockerbrush" conclude with a statement about human nature that is true for Krause's valley as for all of frontier America. Old Pilversack, says the first speaker,

> He's out to gather strays back to the fold—
> Old lady Bursch, Jimiah Glugersfeld.
> Even got the Poger toughs to coming nights.
> Over Loon Lake way they've built 'em platform wagons
> To make the trip.
> Says the second,
> > Time haying weather starts,
> > They'll leave the meetinghouse to mice
> > and squirrels,
> > The way it's always been.

The best verses in *Neighbor Boy* are the short lyrics, six or eight of them—like "Hillside Burial" (the poem that led to the inquiry from Simon and Schuster that encouraged Krause to complete *Wind Without Rain*)—perfect in their own kind as moods and moments peculiar to Pockerbrush as well as universal. Although Krause did not often enough achieve in his lyrics the "stabbing line" that Benét urged him to cultivate, in this passage from "I spittle up my whistle," the preface to *Neighbor Boy*, there is an echo of the rich alliterative verse of *Beowulf* and "The Wanderer":

> Each has a lipful of weather-wind given
> To waste under heaven
> As whistle. So much have I;
> The rest is for waiting. Let there be time to borrow
> Music from the dawn for song tomorrow.

The theme of time and borrowed time is pervasive in Krause's poetry. He was painfully aware that the years had passed him by, that he had started his education four years late, and that his writing genius seemed to be ripening slowly. In a poem that may have caught its title from the lines just quoted, "Song Tomorrow," the theme is patience. The young bird who has just "graduated" from pinfeathers knows enough to learn to sing according to nature's time-scheme. In "Valley Griselda" the persona of the poem, watching the patient frog and the painstaking ant, contemplates even "outsitting a barby rose / Unpettaling red" because it's best to "Learn something of waiting . . . , / By doing some waiting yourself."

The flora and fauna and people of Pockerbrush form the subject matter of all the varied poems in *Neighbor Boy*. There is the sudden coming of the frost, and the dark knowledge that earth takes the laborer as well as his labor. There are poems, too, about madness, like "Strange Boy" and "Calico Come"; about black magic, like "Incantation for a Curse" and "Dark Messenger"; but also about the rich beauty of life lived close to nature, as in "Bunching Hay," "Something to Five," "See What's to See," "Neighbor East-and-North," "Wild Plum Firstling," and "Drowsy Noon." As Paul Engle wrote in his introduction to *Neighbor Boy*, "The diversity of these poems is evidence that the writer knows the diversity of living. One of the virtues of Herbert Krause's book is that it is not enough to look at life clearly, one must also write about it flexibly." With this collection Krause satisfied the deep desire he had had from early childhood on to try to capture in new ways in words and sounds his discoveries in nature and in human life.

VI

The idea for a novel about threshing had also been in Krause's mind for a long time, ever since 1933, when the last of the old-time Hill threshers—Bill Welbrock—had died. By September 1940 Krause was thinking about such a novel and writing to farm equipment manufacturers in order to gather material for *The Thresher*. But the times were wrong for a work by a German-

American, even though Paul Engle—himself of German ancestry—assured Krause that the hatred that was growing in America was toward Hitler and not the German people. The idea remained undeveloped for three more years, until the fall of 1943, when Krause felt compelled to go to work again. His St. Olaf advisor and adopted father, "Pop" Spohn, had died that summer, and that may have been the chief stimulus. Or it may have been the break with an old friend that took place about the same time. By January Krause had formulated his plans thoroughly enough to present them to the University of Minnesota along with the request for a year's Regional Writing Fellowship. In March he received word that he had won one of the $2,700 grants, beginning 1 June 1944. By September he could write to Lawrence Chambers, president of Bobbs-Merrill, that the research was done and he was ready to write. The novel appeared at last in January 1947.

The Thresher is the story of Johnny Black, a man of enormous energy and drive, who attempts to gain complete mastery over his world, that narrow corner of Minnesota that Krause had earlier identified as Pockerbrush. He proves himself to be, as Kristoffer Paulson characterizes him, an embodiment of Frederick Jackson Turner's warning against the expression of excessive individualism on the frontier, "pressing individual liberty beyond its proper bounds ... " ("Ole Rølvaag" 24-25). In rapid succession Johnny attains ownership of one, then two, and finally three steam-powered wheat-threshing rigs, monstrous iron machines with the poetic names "Red Star," "Buffalo Head," and "Golden Bird." By virtue of his determination, ingenuity, and occasional ruthlessness, Johnny beats out his competition and arrives at a position of absolute dominance in the community. In doing so he sacrifices his wife Lilice and his best friend "Snoose" Marchen and sets the stage for his own tragic demise when gasoline-powered tractors and farmers' cooperatives strike a death blow at the very heart of his domain.

Behind much of Johnny's all-consuming ambition lies his conviction as a youth that he has inherited his father's mysterious evil nature. It is a belief drilled into him by his guardian aunt, Phrena Barewolf, out of her deep anger at Johnny's dead father for courting her and then casting her aside. Aunt Phrena is a religious fanatic who intends Johnny for the ministry until he rebels. His sense of guilt is reinforced by Pastor Steuber, a sternly sincere invoker of Old Testament recriminations who refuses to marry Johnny and Lilice Rose after she becomes pregnant. Against these and a gossipping, censorious community Johnny pits his threshing rigs, throwing himself into his work both to prove his true worth and to find forgetfulness for the pain of lost years and friends.

As with *Wind Without Rain*, the reviews of *The Thresher* were on the whole positive, with most critics according the novel a higher place than its predecessor. Once again *The Saturday Review of Literature* printed a highly favorable critique. Nancy Groberg Chaikin wrote, "By strong, poetic writing which fondles its metaphors almost sensually, we are swept, in this story of a man's ambitious drive for power, through the life of a German farm community in Minnesota, and through the life of Johnny Schwartz . . . " (12). The weaknesses, she added, were in Krause's overfondness for metaphor and particularly in his too-obtrusive use of the concept of time. Walter Havighurst's review in the *New York Herald Tribune*, while agreeing that Krause's treatment of time was flawed, argued that the novel is "an urgent, compassionate, uncompromising picture of rural life, which Hamlin Garland would earnestly affirm" (4).

The hint at a comparison with Garland might have pleased Krause, but he must have been delighted at the suggestion in more than one review that he was a successor to the great Norwegian-

American novelist Ole E. Rølvaag. James Gray, as a matter of fact, claimed Rølvaag's mantle for Krause, however loosely it might be cast about him: "Mr. Krause is the interpreter of a Midwestern community of German background; Rølvaag was the interpreter of transplanted Norwegians. All the differences of temperament between the two groups are evident in the rhythm, the pace, the emotional emphasis in the work of the two . . . " (*Chicago Daily News* 6 Jan. 1947).

Besides presenting the life of a frontier German community and telling the tragic story of Johnny Black, Krause had intended *The Thresher* to serve as an authentic document of an important era in the history of farming life in America. Indeed, John T. Frederick's review in the *Chicago Sun* was largely given over to an appreciation of Krause's novel as a contribution to rural social history, particularly, of course, to the evolution of threshing machines and newer methods of harvesting and handling grain. From his own experience, Frederick could report: "[Krause's] treatment of this whole dramatic process of social and economic change—from cradle to binder, from primitive horse-driven thresher to the steam engine and finally the tractor—is sound, complete, and discriminating. For this element alone *The Thresher* would have permanent value" (4). Havighurst, too, noted Krause's treatment of threshing, calling it the most complete in American fiction. When one adds to the authentic picture of threshing an equally authentic picture of the German-American folk-life of the hills, complementing that in *Wind Without Rain*—the country dances, revival meetings, bar-room brawls, school scenes, worship services, and dinner-table conversations—Krause's contribution to American letters takes on a new and unique dimension.

The success of *The Thresher* was of a much different order than had been that of *Wind Without Rain*. While the latter won a prize, its sales were meager, scarcely reaching 11,000. *The Thresher*, on the other hand, won no awards, although many reviewers urged it as a Pulitzer Prize candidate, but it sold almost 400,000 copies through various book clubs, the Armed Forces edition, and bookstore sales. Krause was particularly pleased at its selection as a Junior Literary Guild offering and as a Literary Guild alternate, and in the fall he reported to President Chambers his surprise and delight at learning that Montgomery Ward's fall and winter catalogue would offer *The Thresher* to its mail-order customers: "I am now safely packaged," he wrote, "along with diapers, toothpaste and vitamin products." An abridgment for *Omnibook*, a book digest magazine, swelled the number of *Threshers* by 200,000 more, and translations into German, Norwegian, and Braille followed. His academic career was, of course, enhanced by the appearance of the novel: in the spring Wallace Stegner invited him to teach at Stanford University at very nearly double his Augustana salary. But Krause declined; he had in mind four more novels whose setting was the Midwest, and to move away from his home base, he felt, would be to cut off the source of his inspiration.

VII

In 1939, not long after *Wind Without Rain* had appeared, Victor Lundeen, the Fergus Falls book dealer, had taken Krause fishing on Lake Lida, north of Pockerbrush, and there had suggested to him a novel about the oxcart trains that in the 1850s and 1860s had crossed Minnesota from east to northwest on a sort of transcontinental highway that linked the Pacific Ocean with the Great Lakes and New Orleans. In Minnesota the trail stretched from the northern end of the Mississippi River at St. Paul to Pembina on the Red River of the North, in what is now North Dakota. The topic seemed a promising one, for the trail once travelled by the heavy two-wheeled carts had passed somewhere near Krause's home territory, and the tracks might still exist. Krause tucked the idea away, however, until the beginning of his University of Minnesota Fellowship in 1944. That fall he wrote Chambers that a novel about the Red River oxcarts was already plotted, as were novels about Pembina and about a blizzard in Pockerbrush. By January of 1945 he had decided to make the trail the subject of his next novel, and he wrote to Theodore Blegen that he would finish it in 1946. But as was true of the first two novels, one delay after another—problems of health and finances as well as a demanding teaching load—stretched the project out for nine more years, so long a time that the momentum in readership and sales that he might have gained by more frequent publishing was completely lost.

In the long interval between *The Thresher* (1946) and *The Oxcart Trail* (1954), Krause dug deeply into the literature about the Red River valley, northwestern Minnesota, and the trade in furs and pemmican in the region. He travelled into the north country with a companion and a couple of Cree Indian guides, amassing a total of 2,000 miles in a nineteen-foot canoe as he sought to verify every detail of his research. At the same time he came close to completing still another Pockerbrush novel, this one a short psychological study, *Emma-August*, that he first mentioned in a letter of 11 August 1945. The next summer he outlined the work, characterizing Emma as "an obstreperous creature, as unmanageable as a thresher." Beyond the fact that the time involved was to be 1890-1912 and the locale Pockerbrush, little more of the novel is known. It may be that he had in mind a composite picture of two women in his family whom he admired greatly, his aunt Emma Krause and his paternal grandmother Augusta Richter Krause. By 1952 he had worked it out completely and had written more than a quarter, but only a dozen loose pages now remain among the Krause Papers at Augustana College. During the long interval Krause also began to cultivate an interest in ornithology, natural history, and Western history that would become an obsession with him, almost to the exclusion of other creative work, until his death in 1976.

The Oxcart Trail probably should have been two novels, one a sequel to the other, for the book divides itself into two nearly self-contained halves. Many reviewers were quick to notice that fact, and some even suggested that while the story of Shawnie Dark at St. Paul in 1850 had its historical interest, it was a long and sometimes slow-moving prologue to the story of Shawnie on the 400-mile trail to the Red River. Many of the complications of the first half, "The Village," work themselves out before the trek begins: the secret of Shawnie's flight from the East is revealed (while helping a Black to escape slavery Shawnie killed a constable) and his fear of pursuit is dissipated by then; the development of Shawnie's friendship with Uncle Jebez is completed and the political squabbling in old St. Paul is over at that point.

What is left for "The Trail" is a solution to Shawnie's unrequited love for Debbie Wells and the resolution of the most profound question raised by the novel, whether Chippewa and Sioux Indians—like the youths Willie Bird and Johnny Buffalo—can be Americanized by clean trousers and Christianity. Debbie thinks so and has committed herself to the cause of civilizing the Red Man. Krause, however, is convinced otherwise, and demonstrates his conviction in a series of violent events along the trail when the caravan is caught between the mutually hostile Sioux and Chippewas. Johnny Buffalo kills and scalps his erstwhile friend Willie Bird, and Debbie—hating violence with missionary zeal—is forced to shoot and kill an Indian while protecting the injured Shawnie. With nearly all of her illusions shattered, she is now ready to accept his dream of a home for the two of them beside their special lake in Otter Tail River country.

Against the admitted weaknesses in the story line and love interest of *The Oxcart Trail* must be placed its strengths in historical accuracy and treatment of an overlooked but highly significant era in the development of the commerce and settlement of the Northwest. Some idea of the depth of Krause's research can be gotten from a series of sixteen articles that he published in the *Fergus Falls Journal* between April 1949 and March 1954. In them he cites entries in journals from the 1850s kept by James Fergus and others, and he provides additional information relating to his studies, his trips to the north country, and the discovery of fur trade data from the late eighteenth century. His description of the oxcarts, for example, is meticulously accurate, for he relied on the published recollections of an old driver who remembered one of his journeys in the 1860s with a Red River cart, "a marvel of mechanism," "made of tough, well-seasoned wood without a particle of iron about it . . . " (Fonseca 2).

Although *The Oxcart Trail* was widely reviewed in American newspapers, it was virtually ignored by influential national magazines. A number of reviewers called attention to the novel's chief weakness, a thin plot line. Victor P. Hass, writing in *The New York Times*, said, "looking at it one way, Herbert Krause is 287 pages getting to the subject promised by the title of his novel" (25). And Walter Havighurst, in a review for the *Chicago Tribune*, concluded that *The Oxcart Trail* was "a serious and substantial historical novel in which the carefully researched background is more memorable than the characters" (4 Apr. 1954). The best review of *The Oxcart Trail* in Krause's estimation, best because it saw most clearly the novelist's intent, was that by James Gray in the *New York Herald Tribune*. Besides praising the novel as a great historical pageant, Gray called attention to the hundreds of small details that add up to a close approximation of what life was like in old St. Paul and on the trail: "The important thing about *The Oxcart Trail* is that it offers a new design for the historical novel. Mr. Krause's plan makes room for a vast amount of historical research, each detail of which has been dramatized . . . " (4 Apr. 1954: 5). The problem was, as Krause himself confessed it, that Shawnie's adventures were less interesting than the historical details in *The Oxcart Trail*. Krause considered it a failure, despite the fact that it sold better than most novels that season. The total was only 10,000 and the work won no prizes or book-club sponsors.

VIII

From 1953 until his death in 1976 Krause began to turn his writing energies away from the novel and into other areas of creativity. For a year or two he wrote out a new work about a World War II veteran who returned to Pockerbrush with his Japanese war bride, but a satisfactory ending eluded him and he burned the finished pages. Far more important than these abortive efforts at fiction was an impressive output of essays and articles, many of them of continuing interest to students of Western literature and natural history. In the *Chicago Sun Midwest Christmas Annual* for 1945, for example, appeared his first prose piece in a national publication, an article on traditional Christmas customs in the frontier communities of western Minnesota. It was in essence a concise summary of the richly detailed passages about German folklife in *Wind Without Rain* and *The Thresher*.

About this same time, however, Krause was developing an interest in ornithology that was to take increasing amounts of his energies for the next thirty years. Although he had long been an avid lover of nature and had depicted its variety in the poetry of *Wind Without Rain* and *Neighbor Boy*, a course in ornithology that winter sparked a lifelong interest in further study of birds and writing about them. A series of his essays on birds was printed in 1947 by the *Fergus Falls Daily Journal*, but these reached a limited audience and are little known today. A much greater number of highly technical articles appeared in ornithological journals over the years, and along with them Krause wrote a handful of less specialized pieces that are still of interest to students of the West. A 1956 essay on the history of ornithology in South Dakota points to J. B. Trudeau's *Journal* of 1794 as the first written record of birds in the state, proceeds to Pierre-Antoine Tabeau, 1803, as the first man to describe South Dakota birds in some detail, and follows these two with a succession of reports by visitors to the state that reaches its climax with John James Audubon in 1843 ("Ornithology in South Dakota").

Krause followed that short essay with two longer pieces on the Major Stephen Long expedition of 1823 into western Minnesota and eastern North Dakota. Published in the fall of 1956 and the spring of 1957, the essays review Long's reports of the birds and animals sighted or shot as game on the journey from the Mississippi River at Prairie du Chien to Pembina in the far northeast corner of what is now North Dakota. While Krause's interest is primarily in the birds and animals of these northern woods and prairies, he notes with a detective's satisfaction that the real reason for the Long Expedition was to ascertain and fix the boundaries between the United States and Canada, and to determine how secure the area was against hostile Indians, or anybody else. Long's conclusion, as Krause notes it, was that the northern frontier, a region "the most dreary imaginable," would "always remain secure from the inroads of any regular hostile force in that direction" ("Ornithology of the Major Long Expedition" 42).

In the mid-sixties Krause published three substantive essays on the ornithology of the Great Plains. Two of these appeared as chapters in Olin Pettingill's *The Bird Watcher's America*, and the third—the most general of the three—in *South Dakota Bird Notes*. In this latter piece, after reviewing the early travelers' reports of the plains as a paradise for game, Krause offers a bitter summation of the present situation: many species lost to the region or to specific areas, and population numbers drastically reduced. The two chapters in *The Bird Watcher's America* are less polemical and much more poetic. In them Krause celebrates the mysterious seasonal flights of legions of Blue, Snow, and Canada Geese along the Missouri; and he surveys what Colonel Dodge called "the wildest and most mysterious of the unknown regions" of the West, the Black Hills of South Dakota. By including entertaining vignettes of his own experiences and enlivening his accounts with figures of speech, Krause invites the reader to enter emotionally as well as intellectually into the magic of migration and the mystery of the Hills. Pettingill's praise of Krause is understated: "Few people I know can match his smooth-flowing descriptive style and meaty anecdotes" ("The Black Hills" 144).

Although Krause's literary criticism was small in quantity by comparison, two valuable essays appeared in the mid-1960s. The earlier of the two, published in the initial number of the *South Dakota Review* in 1963, is a brilliant review of the appearance of the cowboy in history and literature. Krause begins with the origins of the word *cowboy*, its earliest appearance in print in America in 1775, and follows it to its first use in the West, in Texas in the 1830s where Cameron's Cowboys rounded up herds of wild longhorns. From there, Krause points out, the idea of cowboy changed, taking on strong characteristics of the Mexican vaquero and attaining early fame in the hands of William Cody, Theodore Roosevelt, and Owen Wister. What gave the cowboy the image of a stoic gunslinger intrigued Krause most of all; among the many causative factors, one stood uppermost in his mind, the harsh Western environment. The cowboy, Krause concludes, "behaved as the desert behaved—indifferent, and inscrutable, when need be." "Like the rattle-snake buzzing its warning, he kept up a tension of deadliness, a warning of imminent disaster" ("Myth" 17).

Much less known than the *SDR* article but as valuable is Krause's later piece on humor on the American frontier. Published in *Verge* magazine in the Philippines while Krause was there as a Rockefeller lecturer in Western literature, "The Half-Horse Alligator: Humor on the American Frontier" tracks the tall tale to its remotest origins in New England and then follows it across the West and into the outrageous hyperboles of modern American advertising. Krause finds the earliest examples of exaggerated stories in the reports from the American colonizers to their constituents in England, but he traces the tall tale proper, with its "swift play of the imagination behind the casual words which harness small facts to mountainous inventions," to Benjamin Franklin, whose whales pursue codfish up Niagara Falls and whose sheep are so woolly that their tails are supported by little four-wheeled wagons (31). Krause concludes that from New England the tall tale moved west, influenced by the hardships of frontier life, by the exaggerated geography of the West and its abundant wild animals, by the power of the steamboat and steam engine, and by regional and ethnic differences among the pioneers.

IX

Krause never gave up his love of poetry and drama, and in 1958 and 1960 produced his two most ambitious works since *Bondsmen to the Hills* and *Neighbor Boy*. The earlier, a long heroic poem, is a tribute to the state of Minnesota called *Giant in the Wooded Earth*. Commissioned as a part of the state's Centennial year, the 121-line tribute was delivered at the University of Minnesota's Memorial Stadium by actor Walter Abel, with background music performed by the Minneapolis Symphony Orchestra. The poem was well-suited to the occasion, for it gave Krause the opportunity to bring his deep interest in Western history together with his gift for powerful and original figures of speech. Minnesota is a "giant ribboned with the silver rush of rivers," whose history of Indian and white relations began with the fur trade, "the shining peltries, gold that ran on padded feet." Then came "emigration's surges," "the locust flood that westward washed" and left "The teepees starving, winter's bony finger sharpening the scalping knife." But now, with this great evil past, Krause saw Minnesota—with its industrial capacity, its scientific genius, and its other intellectual potentialities—as poised with the rest of America to enter a new frontier, the galaxy. The poem concludes:

> Go, Strider of the Satellite Age, twirl lariats of
> > rocket-flame,
> and through the luna dark hurl shining ropes to
> > loop the utmost coruscating star.

The powerful optimism, appropriate for the occasion no doubt, stands in strong contrast to Krause's deep pessimism—expressed elsewhere—about America's ability to manage its natural resources, about the continued mistreatment of the Indian, and indeed about human nature itself, which Krause saw as radically flawed.

The last important creative work in which Krause engaged himself was the script for an outdoor pageant called *Crazy Horse*, his only full-length treatment of an Indian subject and only his second effort at drama. The decision to write about the life and death of the nineteenth-century Indian hero and the ignominious end of his Oglala Sioux people was a natural outgrowth of Krause's interest in Western American history. What Krause envisioned in his drama was epic in scope and realistic to the last detail of Sioux Indian and frontier life, full of vigorous action and spectacular effects and according closely with events on the Western plains from the 1850s to the 1870s. He had in mind an outdoor setting at the base of the Black Hills with room for a log fort, several tipis, and space for up to ten horses to maneuver.

The heroic effect that Krause aims at includes a great issue—a whole people and their unique way of life about to be destroyed—along with battles, journeys, a singular hero, and even the intervention of the gods. From beginning to end, Crazy Horse is at the center of the action. His earliest contacts with the whites are threatening to him and reach an early high point with the Grattan massacre. Not long after, while Crazy Horse is away on the vision quest that he hopes will determine his calling, General Harney attacks his village. On Crazy Horse's return to the scene of the massacre, he experiences an overwhelming vision that commits him to the rescue of his people. Many successes in battle follow, climaxed by the Indians' rubbing out of Custer at the Little Big Horn. But from this point on Crazy Horse becomes the acted upon rather than the actor. He is arrested at Fort Robinson, betrayed by his own people as well as by the military, and is shot to death when he attempts to flee. The medicine man, who has functioned much like a Greek chorus throughout, pronounces the last rites on Crazy Horse but also on all the Indian people.

The idea of an outdoor pageant was shelved in 1960, however, and the problems presented by the production of *Crazy Horse* have left it unperformed up to the present. A changing climate of opinion toward the portrayal of Indian people on stage and screen will make an eventual production of the play a certainty; and improvements in sound amplification and lighting over the past quarter century should ensure a successful performance in either an outdoor or indoor setting.

X

From 1961, when he was awarded a Fulbright lectureship in South Africa, until 1969, when he returned from a three-year Rockefeller professorship in the Philippines, Krause produced no creative work of length beyond the essays discussed earlier. He started a book on the bald eagle for McGraw-Hill, but held up the final chapters because new legislation was beginning to ameliorate the environmental effects of DDT and other toxins, and the work remains unfinished. Without question Krause believed that the most important accomplishment in these last years was the establishing of the Center for Western Studies at Augustana College. The idea of a center for regional study at the college had helped to attract him there in 1938 when he and President Clemens M. Granskou had agreed that an important task for Krause at Augustana would be the training of young writers from the area to appreciate their heritage. The idea was never allowed to die, and in 1959, when he was preparing to write *Crazy Horse* by studying the religion of the Sioux Indians, Krause began to think seriously about a new model for regional study, a center where information about historic and prehistoric peoples could be gotten at easily. In 1969 the Center was organized and in April 1970 Krause officially became the director.

By 1974, while he was suffering health problems of increasing severity, the Center was awarded a substantial grant from the National Endowment for the Humanities for an innovative program that was designed to bring Augustana's faculty and students to a clearer understanding of the American West. Within a few weeks of the announcement of the grant, the Center organized a testimonial dinner for Krause, with Frederick Manfred and longtime friend Pat Blegen as speakers and with J. Earl Lee playing the piano for Krause as he had done so very often ever since Krause's arrival at Augustana in 1938. The dinner was also the occasion for the publication of Krause's last major work (edited with history professor Gary D. Olson), *Prelude to Glory*, the story of Custer's 1874 incursion into the Black Hills in the words of the reporters who accompanied what was called a scientific expedition to the sacred lands of the Sioux and the Cheyenne but what was probably intended by Custer to advance his political ambitions.

Krause's "Introduction" to *Prelude to Glory* points out that the Black Hills was unexplored in 1874 when General Philip Sheridan issued the letter of commission to Brigadier General A. H. Terry, commander of the Department of Dakota, directing him to send an expedition under Lieutenant Colonel G. A. Custer to "that unknown section of the country" (1). In addition to the ten companies of the Seventh Cavalry, Custer took with him three companies of infantry, a battery of Gatling guns, and one hundred Arikara scouts under the famous Bloody Knife. In case of trouble with the Sioux, he intended to be fully prepared. Moreover, Krause points out, Custer took with him correspondents for six newspapers and made certain that their reports would include information about the fertile soil and hints of mineral wealth that lay along the trail. When the news broke on 27 August that gold had been discovered in the Black Hills, it was no more than what Custer had expected. Krause suggests in his "Epilogue" that the colonel intended to promote himself as fully as possible through the newspapers, perhaps with some longer-range political objective in mind. The expedition, however, and the gold rush that followed, resulted in Indian grievances that are still being contested today.

While the reviews of *Prelude to Glory* were fewer in number than those for any of Krause's novels, they were uniformly favorable. Laurence A. Jolidon, for example, writing in the *Detroit Free Press*, calls the book "exactly the backdrop needed to sense the main elements: the rugged self-importance of everyone on the expedition, including the scientists and the writers; the total lack of regard for Indian rights and culture; an unrelenting faith in the benefits of white settlement" (1, 4). A review by Carl R. Baldwin in the *St. Louis Post-Dispatch*, after calling the book "a masterpiece of sorts," points to the language used by the correspondents in writing about the Indians as evidence of pervasive racism in American society. For correspondent Nathan H. Knappen of the *Bismarck Tribune* the Indian was "poor Lo," a sarcastic use of Alexander Pope's line in *An Essay on Man*, "Lo, the poor Indian! whose untutored mind / Sees God in clouds, or hears him in the wind." Correspondent Aris B. Donaldson of the *St. Paul Pioneer* called the Indian "the depraved nomad," and William E. Curtis, who wrote for both the *Chicago Inter-Ocean* and the *New York World*, spoke of the Sioux "infesting" the Black Hills. Besides its value in adding depth to an important chapter in Custer's career, *Prelude to Glory* helps the reader to understand the climate of opinion in 1874 that made Custer's recommendation so very palatable to millions of Americans: "The extinguishment of the Indian title to the Black Hills and the establishment of a military post in the vicinity of Harney's Peak and another at some good point on the Little Missouri will settle the Indian question so far as the Northwest is concerned" (237).

XI

What Herbert Krause had sought to do from the beginning of his writing career to the end, particularly in his novels *Wind Without Rain* and *The Thresher*, was to find the most honest way to express the West, to discover its most honest language and its distinctive metaphor. As he wrote to former student Greg Beaumont in 1966:

> The charge is always the same: the West is bleak and barren; it is uncouth, its people uncultured, its culture skin deep and six-gun: scratch a Western and you reveal a tomahawk. Van Wyck Brooks said so; the West killed Mark Twain, the artist, he said; therefore it must be so. But it isn't so. I felt when I wrote *The Thresher* and I feel now that what was needed were images that had nothing to do with the Hudson River or the Kaatskills. The West must be expressed in the imagery of its environment; an indigenous imagery in rock and grasshopper, in pebble and mountain lookout. Walter Channing complained about eastern American writers as far back as 1815 (in *North American Review*) that they were attempting to describe "the majesty of the Mississippi" in language "which was made for the Thames." It is still true today.

Herbert Krause's contribution to the "metaphor" of the novel of the American West is twofold: a new and more intense poetry in the telling of the story of a people, and a powerful evocation of a region in the West that had been neglected in fiction as well as in history. In *Wind Without Rain* Krause asserted that no person and no people—not even the remote and impoverished Germans of Friberg—are unimportant, and no place and no suffering are unaccompanied by beauty. In *The Thresher* he recreated the most significant era of transition in the history of mankind's growing and harvesting of grain, the time when hand labor and horse labor capitulated to steam power and the gasoline tractor in a matter of only a few decades. And in *The Oxcart Trail* Krause offered an awesome example of research in the historical novel, for *The Oxcart Trail* rests on a base of fact, accurate and complete; and it tells the story of that short but important period in the mid-nineteenth century when trains of handmade carts, each with its ox and its half-breed driver, formed a long and tenuous link between the Pacific on the one hand and the Gulf of Mexico and the Atlantic Ocean on the other. Krause's choice of the metaphor "giant in the wooded earth" comes as close perhaps as any to identifying the Minnesota experience, and it recalls as well another Minnesotan whose giants were of a different earth, but not a more powerful or significant one.

Selected Bibliography

The listing below includes all of Krause's major published literary work, selections of his numerous poems, essays and reviews, and selected secondary source material, including reviews. The latter number in the hundreds, although many are brief notices.

PRIMARY SOURCES

Books

Der Drescher. Berlin: Volksberband der Bücherfreunde Wegweiser-Verlag, [1950]. (German translation of *The Thresher*)

Fiction 151-1, Short Stories. Preface by Carlos P. Romulo. Ed. with afterword by Herbert Krause. Manila: MDB Publishing House, 1968.

An Index to South Dakota Bird Notes: Official Publication of South Dakota Ornithologists' Union, volumes 1-5 [Sioux Falls, 1954].

Neighbor Boy. Iowa City, Ia.: Midland House, 1939.

The Oxcart Trail. Indianapolis: Bobbs-Merrill, 1954; rpt. Sioux Falls: Brevet Press, 1976.

Prelude to Glory: A Newspaper Accounting of Custer's 1874 Expedition to the Black Hills. Ed. with Gary D. Olson. Sioux Falls: Brevet Press, 1974.

The Thresher. Indianapolis: Bobbs-Merrill, 1946; rpt. Sioux Falls: Brevet Press, 1976.

Wind Without Rain. Indianapolis: Bobbs-Merrill, 1939; rpt. Sioux Falls: Brevet Press, 1976.

Short Stories

"Horning in the Fall." *Eve's Stepchildren*. Ed. Lealon N. Jones. Caldwell, Ida.: The Caxton Printers, 1942. 150-61.

"The Oak Tree." *Prairie Prose* 1 (Winter 1943): 3-7.

Essays, Articles, Reviews

Rev. of *Adventure Lit Their Star*, by Kenneth Allsop. *The Wilson Bulletin* 78 (1966): 246-48.

[Autobiographical sketch.] *Minnesota Writers*. Ed. Carmen Nelson Richards. Minneapolis: T. S. Denison, 1961. 19-27.

"The Black Hills of South Dakota." *Audubon Magazine* 67 (May-June 1965): 140, 142-45.

"The Black Hills of South Dakota." *The Bird Watcher's America*. Ed. Olin Sewall Pettingill, Jr. New York: McGraw-Hill, 1965. 143-51.

"Clear Light of Children's Joys Shines on in Memory." *The Chicago Sun Book Week* 2 Dec. 1945: 57. (Christmas in Pockerbrush)

"Farmers in Literature." Rev. of *The Middle Western Farm Novel in the Twentieth Century*, by Roy W. Meyer. *Minnesota History* 39 (1965): 293.

"The Frontier in American History." *National Audubon Society Proceedings*, 60th Annual Convention. 7-11 Nov. 1964, Tucson, Arizona, 15-16.

"Geese Along the Missouri." *The Bird Watcher's America*. Ed. Olin Sewall Pettingill. New York: McGraw-Hill, 1965. 365-70.

Rev. of *Grass of the Earth: Immigrant Life in the Dakota Country*, by Aagot Raaen. *Minnesota History* 32 (1951): 52-53.

"The Half-Horse Alligator: Humor on the American Frontier." *Verge* (University of the Philippines) 2 (1966): 15-37.

"The McCown's Longspur." *Life Histories of North American Cardinals, Grosbeaks, Buntings, Towhees, Finches, Sparrows, and Allies . . . .* Ed. Arthur Cleveland Bent. Washington: Smithsonian Institution Press, 1968. 1564-97.

"Mammals of the Major Long Expedition, 1823." *Minnesota Naturalist* 8 (1957): 1-4.

"Myth and Reality on the High Plains." *The South Dakota Review* 1 (1963): 3-20.

"Nesting of a Pair of Canada Warblers." *The Living Bird* 4 (1965): 5-11.

"A Note on Accuracy." *The Messenger* (Sioux Falls) 23 (1939): 12-13.

"A Note on the Possibilities of South Dakota Writing." *English Notes* (South Dakota) 1 (1955): 1-3.

"Ornithology in South Dakota Before Audubon." *South Dakota Academy of Science, Proceedings* 35 (1956): 198-201.

"The Ornithology of the Great Plains with Special Reference to South Dakota." *South Dakota Bird Notes* 16 (1964): 12-21.

"Ornithology of the Major Long Expedition, 1823." *Minnesota Naturalist* 7 (1956): 39-42.

"The Reach and the Grasp." *South Dakota Education Association Journal* 18 (1942): 120-21.

"Spirit of West Lives on in Book." Review of *The Tree of Bones*, by John R. Milton. *Minneapolis Tribune, Book Section* 8 Aug. 1965: 8.

"Trailing Lewis and Clark." *Audubon Magazine* 68 (1966): 78-80.

"The Trouble That Poetry Has." *South Dakota Education Association Journal* 19 (1944): 297.

Poetry

"The Builder and the Stone, A Salute to Lawrence M. Stavig." Sioux Falls, [1959].

"The Crucifixion." *Lutheran Herald* 4 June 1929: 808.

"Early April Day." *St. Olaf Quarterly* 11 (1934): 48.

"Giant in the Wooded Earth—Minnesota Centennial Verses." *St. Olaf Alumnus* 10 (1962): 3-7.

"Harvest." In *American States Anthology—1934*. New York: The Galleon Press, 1935. 435.

"In Memory of Robert Frost." *The Augustana College Alumnus* 4 (1963): 2.

"The New Cathay: A Salute to Charles Lewis Balcer on the Occasion of His Inauguration as the Sixteenth President of Augustana College." Sioux Falls, 1965.

"Pockerbrush Patches." *The Crust: Bread Loaf School Year Book*. Middlebury: 1935. 30-31, 64-68 (five poems).

"The Telephone, A Narrative Poem." *The Parchment* 3 (1932): 42-45.

Unpublished Works

"Bondsmen to the Hills." One-act play. [1934].

Crazy Horse: A Drama of the Plains Indian and the Black Hills. [Sioux Falls, 1960].

"Pockerbrush." M.A. Thesis Univ. of Iowa, 1935.

Bibliography

Dunmire, Raymond V., compiler. *The Herbert Krause Collection Bibliography.* Vol. 1 (1975); vol. 2 (1976). Sioux Falls, South Dakota: Augustana College Mikkelsen Library and Learning Resources Center.

Archives

The Herbert Krause Papers. Letters, manuscripts, galley proofs, photos, notes, class lectures, and the Krause Collection of Western Americana are in the Center for Western Studies, Augustana College, Sioux Falls, South Dakota.

SECONDARY SOURCES

Baldwin, Carl R. "What Custer Was After." *St. Louis Post-Dispatch* 25 Aug. 1974, sec. B: 4.

Barry, Iris. "Told with Veracity and Power." *New York Herald Tribune Books* 12 Feb. 1939: 5.

Baylor, Leslie M. "The Functions of Nature in Herbert Krause's Pockerbrush Novels." M. A. Thesis Idaho State Univ., 1965.

Beresford, J. D. "Books of the Day: Four New Novels." *Manchester Guardian* 7 July 1939: 7.

Borgenicht, Miriam. "Wind Without Rain." *The New Republic* 8 Mar. 1939: 144.

Chaikin, Nancy Groberg. "A Man's Drive for Power." *Saturday Review of Literature* 8 Feb. 1947: 12.

Christensen, Vi Ann Sattre. "The German Immigrant as Portrayed in the Novels of Herbert Krause." M. A. Thesis Mankato State College, 1968.

Church, Richard. "New Novels to Read: Herbert Krause's Long Tale of a Family in Minnesota." *John O'London's Weekly* 14 July 1939: 531-32.

Connole, John M. "The Oxcart Trail." *America, National Catholic Weekly Review* 5 June 1954: 282.

Derleth, August. "Orphan's Life with Midwest Thresher Ring." *Chicago Tribune* 5 Jan. 1947: 4.

Fadiman, Clifton. "Books." *The New Yorker* 11 Feb. 1939: 72-73.

"A First Novel Gets Friends of Writers Award." *Chicago Daily Tribune* 17 Mar. 1939: 22.

Flanagan, John T. "Frontier in Fiction." *Minnesota History* 34 (1954): 123-24.

──────── . "Thirty Years of American Fiction." *Minnesota History* 31 (1950): 129-47.

Fonseca, W. G. "On the St. Paul Trail in the Sixties." *The Historical and Scientific Society of Manitoba* 56. (25 Jan. 1900). Winnipeg: Manitoba Free Press Company. 2.

Frederick, John T. "When a Poet Writes About a Farmer." *Chicago Sun Book Week* 19 Jan. 1947: 4.

Gannett, Lewis. "Books and Things." *New York Herald Tribune* 15 Feb. 1939: 15.

Gray, James. "Herbert Krause Takes Mantle of O. E. Rølvaag." *Chicago Daily News* 6 Jan. 1947.

——————. "Liquor, Love and Brawling on the Long Road Westward." *New York Herald Tribune Book Review* 4 Apr. 1954: 5.

Hass, Victor P. "A Yankee in Minnesota." *New York Times Book Review* 11 Apr. 1954: 25.

Havighurst, Walter. "Driving Force on the Prairie." *New York Herald Tribune Weekly Book Review* 12 Jan. 1947: 4.

——————. "Vigorous Days on the Old Red River Trail." *Chicago Tribune* 4 Apr. 1954.

Janssen, Judith M. "Black Frost in Summer: Central Themes in the Novels of Herbert Krause." *South Dakota Review* 5 (1967): 55-65.

Jolidon, Laurence A. "Riding with Custer—Aug. 1874." *Detroit Free Press* 18 Aug. 1974: D: 1, 4.

[Klausler, Alfred]. "Dostoevsky in Minnesota." *The Cresset* 2 (Mar. 1939): 47-49.

McKenna, John B. "Newspapermen Record Custer on One Successful Campaign." *The Sunday Oregonian* 6 Oct. 1974, sec. 2: 21.

Mair, John. "New Novels." *The New Statesman and Nation* (London) 15 July 1939: 90.

Metzger, Bill. "The Man Who Created Pockerbrush." *State College Dakotan* 8 (1958): 3-4, 14.

Meyer, Roy W. *The Middle Western Farm Novel in the Twentieth Century*. Lincoln: University of Nebraska Press, 1965.

——————. "Herbert Krause." *A Bibliographical Guide to Midwestern Literature*. Ed. Gerald Nemanic. Iowa City: Univ. of Iowa Press, 1981. 267-69.

North, Sterling. "Books of the Week." *The Chicago Daily News* 15 Feb. 1939: 10.

Nute, Grace Lee. *A History of Minnesota Books and Authors*. Minneapolis: Univ. of Minnesota Press, 1958.

Paulson, Kristoffer F. "Krause, Herbert (Arthur)." *Twentieth-Century Western Writers*. Ed. James Vinson. Detroit: Gale Research Co., 1982. 463-65.

——————. "Ole Rølvaag, Herbert Krause, and the Frontier Thesis of Frederick Jackson Turner." *Where the West Begins*. Ed. Arthur R. Huseboe and William Geyer. Sioux Falls: Center for Western Studies Press, 1978. 24-33.

Rascoe, Burton. "Ad Lib." *Newsweek* 27 Feb. 1939: 36.

Salomon, Louis B. "Tragedy in Minnesota." *The Nation* 18 Feb. 1939: 208.

Solovskoy, Valborg Berge. "The World of Nature in the Writings of Herbert Krause." M. S. Thesis Mankato State College, 1973.

Steensma, Robert C. "'Our Comings and Our Goings': Herbert Krause's *Wind Without Rain*." In *Where the West Begins*. Ed. Arthur R. Huseboe and William Geyer. Sioux Falls: Center for Western Studies Press, 1978. 13-22.

Stegner, Wallace. "A Strong Novel of the Minnesota Land." *Saturday Review of Literature* 11 Feb. 1939: 5.

Upton, Barbara Roberts. "A Study of the Works of Herbert Krause with Special Emphasis on *The Thresher*." M. S. Thesis Mankato State College, 1963.

Wallace, Margaret. "*Wind Without Rain* and Other Recent Works of Fiction." *New York Times Book Review* 12 Feb. 1939: 6.

Wilburs, Stephen. *The Iowa Writers' Workshop*. Iowa City: The Univ. of Iowa, 1980.

"*Wind Without Rain*." (London) *Times Literary Supplement* 15 July 1939: 419.

Huseb
Huseboe, Arthur R., 1931-
Herbert Krause